T0375939

GERM INVADERS
BATTLING EAR, NOSE, AND THROAT INFECTIONS

ELSIE OLSON

Big Buddy Books

An Imprint of Abdo Publishing
abdobooks.com

abdobooks.com

Published by Abdo Publishing, a division of ABDO, PO Box 398166, Minneapolis, Minnesota 55439. Copyright © 2021 by Abdo Consulting Group, Inc. International copyrights reserved in all countries. No part of this book may be reproduced in any form without written permission from the publisher. Big Buddy Books™ is a trademark and logo of Abdo Publishing.

Printed in the United States of America, North Mankato, Minnesota
102020
012021

Design: Sarah DeYoung, Mighty Media, Inc.
Production: Mighty Media, Inc.
Editor: Rebecca Felix

Cover Photographs: Dan Higgins - Medical Illustrator/Centers for Disease Control and Prevention (bacteria); Shutterstock (nurse)
Interior Photographs: Shutterstock (all)
Design Elements: Shutterstock (all)

Library of Congress Control Number: 2020940278

Publisher's Cataloging-in-Publication Data
Names: Olson, Elsie, author.
Title: Battling ear, nose, and throat infections / by Elsie Olson
Description: Minneapolis, Minnesota : Abdo Publishing, 2021 | Series: Germ invaders | Includes online resources and index
Identifiers: ISBN 9781532194214 (lib. bdg.) | ISBN 9781098213572 (ebook)
Subjects: LCSH: Ear, nose, and throat diseases--Juvenile literature. | Health behavior--Juvenile literature. | Science--Experiments--Juvenile literature. | Viruses--Juvenile literature. | Medicine, Preventive--Juvenile literature. | Otolaryngology--Juvenile literature.
Classification: DDC 616.079--dc23

CONTENTS

Your Amazing Body..4

When Germs Attack Your Ears, Nose,
    and Throat..6

All about Your Ears, Nose, and Throat 8

When Germs Invade: Ears...............................10

Ear Trouble 14

When Germs Invade: Nose...............................16

Adenoid Trouble.. 20

When Germs Invade: Throat.............................22

Tonsil Trouble 26

Healthy Habits..28

Glossary 30

Online Resources 31

Index..32

YOUR AMAZING BODY

You are amazing! So is your body. Most of the time your body works just fine. But sometimes germs **invade** it. Germs can make you sick. Every year, millions of people get ear, nose, and throat (ENT) **infections**.

GET TO KNOW GERMS

Germs are tiny **organisms**. They can live inside people, plants, and animals. There are four main types of germs.

VIRUSES

Viruses are parasitic. This means they cannot survive on their own. They require a host cell to reproduce.

BACTERIA

Bacteria are single-celled creatures. They can survive on their own or inside another living organism.

PROTOZOA

Protozoa are single-celled creatures. Some can survive on their own. Others are parasitic.

FUNGI

Fungi are plant-like organisms. They get their food from people, plants, and animals.

WHEN GERMS ATTACK YOUR EARS, NOSE, AND THROAT

Most ENT **infections** are caused by viruses or bacteria. Sore throats and **sinus** infections can be **contagious**. Ear infections are not. But they are a **complication** of colds, which are contagious. Germs causing colds spread easily.

INVASION

A sick person near you coughs or sneezes, sending germs into the air. You breathe in the germ.

FINDING A HOST

The germ attaches to a host cell inside your nose or throat.

REPLICATION

A germ sends out its **genetic** material into the host cell. It orders the cell to make copies of the virus. A bacterium uses a host cell only for nutrients. It makes copies on its own.

SPREADING

The germ's copies spread throughout your body. Any time you cough or sneeze, you send germs into the air. Now the illness can **infect** other people.

FIGHTING BACK

Your immune system notices the infection and fights back.
- White blood cells attack the **invading** germ.
- Your body temperature may increase, causing a fever. This helps kill the germs.

ALL ABOUT YOUR EARS, NOSE, AND THROAT

Your ears let you hear the world around you. Your nose provides your sense of smell. It also plays a role in your sense of taste.

Your throat provides a path for air to reach your lungs. It also provides a route for water and food to reach your stomach.

8

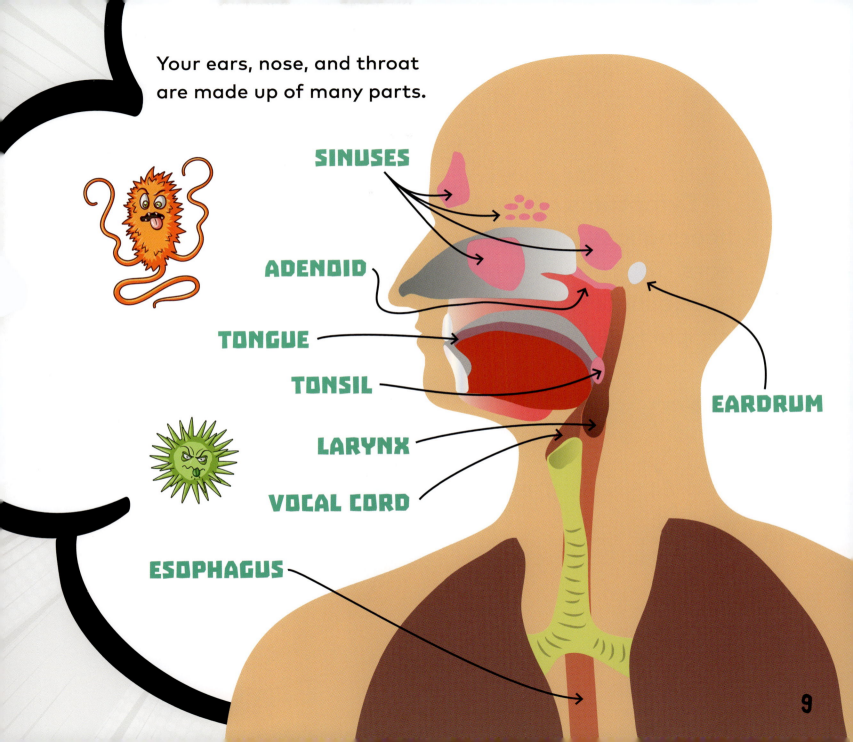

WHEN GERMS INVADE: EARS

Symptoms of ear **infections** include ear pain, hearing loss, and redness or swelling in the ears. You may also have a fever, dizziness, or a headache. Fluid may drain from your ear. Some people feel as if there is water stuck in their ears!

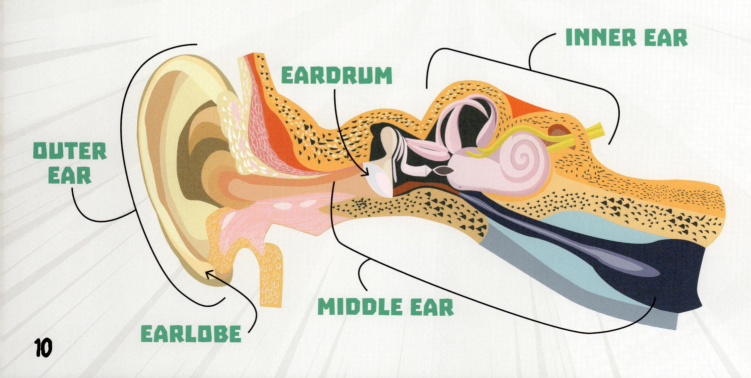

Kids get ear infections more often than adults. This is because certain tubes in kids' ears are still developing and don't drain very well.

Treating ear **infections** depends on the germ causing it. Call your doctor if you have any ear infection **symptoms**. The doctor can determine if a virus or bacteria is causing it.

If it's a virus, **over-the-counter** medicines can ease pain. Bacterial infections can be treated with **antibiotics** from your doctor.

SCIENCE BREAKTHROUGH

In the 1920s, Scottish scientist Alexander Fleming accidentally grew a strange mold. The mold produced a substance that could kill bacteria. He named the substance penicillin. This was the first antibiotic!

Some doctors specialize in ENT infections. These doctors are called otolaryngologists.

EAR TROUBLE

Ear **infections** may cause serious problems. **Pus** may build up. Too much pus can tear or burst your eardrum. This is painful! The eardrum usually heals on its own. But **surgery** may be needed.

Some kids have **chronic** ear infections. Their doctors may perform surgery to place a plastic or metal tube in the eardrum. The tube helps fluid drain out of the ear.

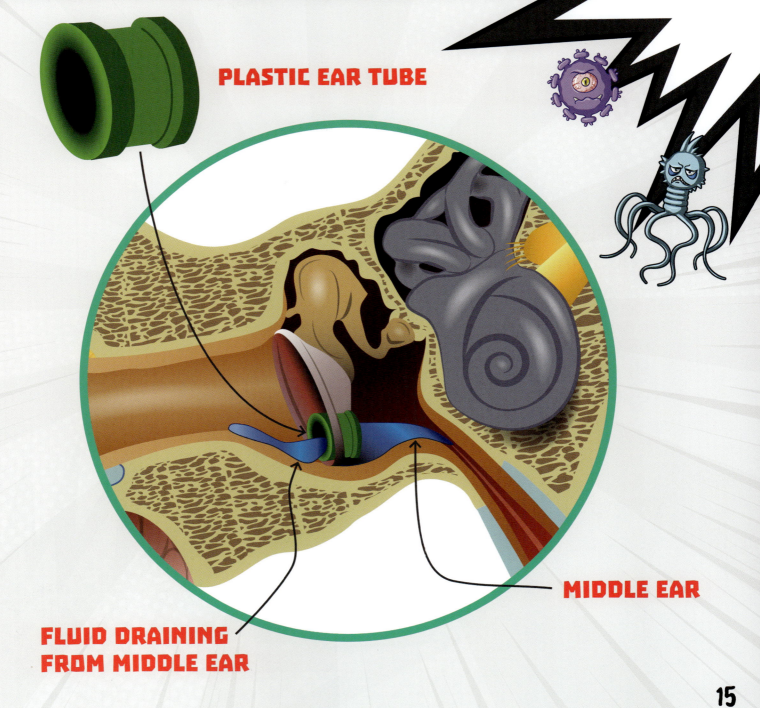

WHEN GERMS INVADE: NOSE

A cold or flu can cause nasal **infections**. **Symptoms** include **congestion**, runny nose, coughing, and sneezing.

Nasal infections may cause your **sinuses** to swell. This is called sinusitis. Sinusitis may cause pain or pressure around your forehead, nose, eyes, and cheeks.

Sinusitis can cause a person to lose their senses of smell and taste while they are sick.

Most people recover from a cold or flu on their own. If you have one of these illnesses, get plenty of rest. And drink lots of fluids. **Over-the-counter** medicines can ease **symptoms**.

But sinusitis may require a doctor visit. Only your doctor will know what type of **infection** you have. Call your doctor if you have symptoms of sinusitis.

ADENOID TROUBLE

Infections can cause trouble in your adenoids. These are folds of tissue at the back of your nasal **cavity**. Germs can cause adenoids to swell, leading to an infection. **Symptoms** include difficulty breathing through the nose and swollen neck glands.

Your doctor may treat the infection with **antibiotics**. But sometimes, the adenoids must be removed through **surgery**.

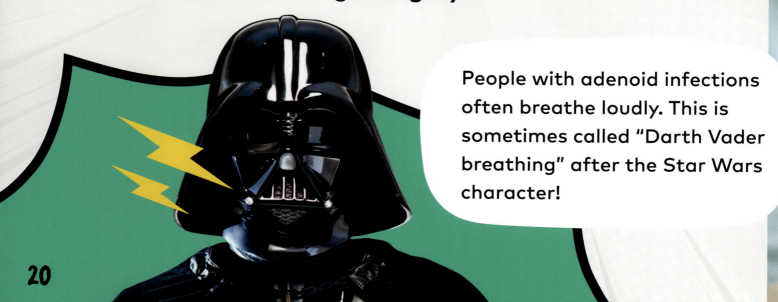

People with adenoid infections often breathe loudly. This is sometimes called "Darth Vader breathing" after the Star Wars character!

WHEN GERMS INVADE: THROAT

Cold and flu viruses are the cause of many sore throats. These viruses can make your throat feel dry or raw.

Your immune system can usually heal a viral **infection** without help. But your doctor might suggest medications. **Over-the-counter** medicines may ease **symptoms**.

A sore throat can make swallowing painful.

Not all sore throats are caused by viruses. A bacteria called *group A Streptococcus* causes the illness strep throat.

Fever, painful swallowing, and swollen **tonsils** are **symptoms** of strep throat. Call your doctor if you experience these symptoms. The doctor can test for the bacteria and treat you with **antibiotics**.

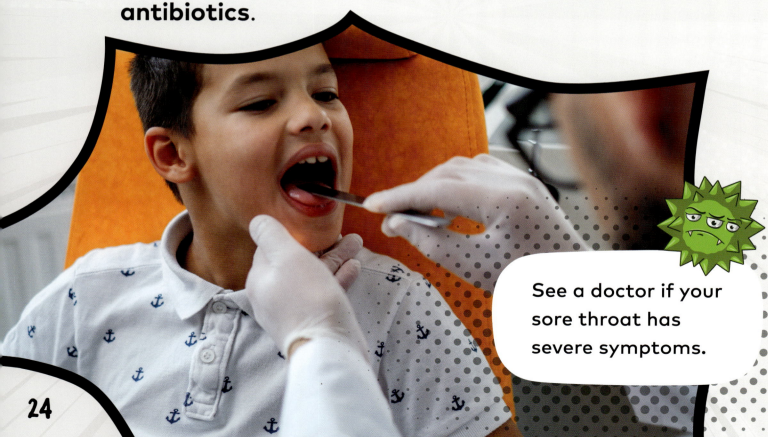

See a doctor if your sore throat has severe symptoms.

SORE THROAT 	STREP THROAT
CAUSE Usually a virus	**CAUSE** Bacteria
SYMPTOMS Coughing, sneezing, runny nose, headache, fever, reduced smell and taste	**SYMPTOMS** Fever, swollen glands, red **tonsils** with white spots, stomach pain
TREATMENT Pain medicine or home **remedies**	**TREATMENT** Antibiotics

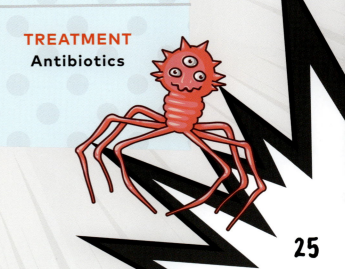

25

TONSIL TROUBLE

Some germs cause **infections** of the **tonsils**. This is called tonsillitis. **Symptoms** include red tonsils with white or yellow spots. You may also have bad breath, ear pain, or a fever.

Some people have **chronic** tonsillitis. They may need **surgery** to remove their tonsils. It can take 10 to 14 days to recover from this surgery.

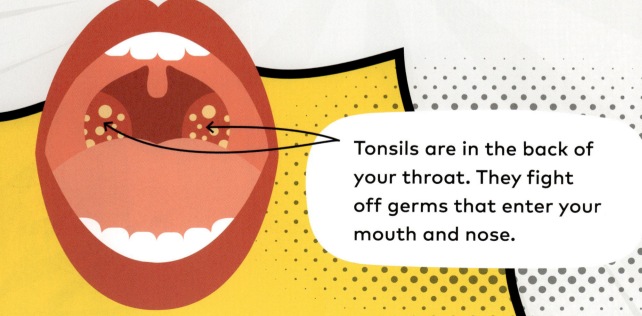

Tonsils are in the back of your throat. They fight off germs that enter your mouth and nose.

HEALTHY HABITS

Healthy habits can help prevent you from getting sick with an ENT **infection**.

- ☐ Keep a safe distance from sick people.
- ☐ Wash your hands often for at least 20 seconds with soap and water.
- ☐ Avoid touching your face.
- ☐ Cough and sneeze into tissues or your elbow.
- ☐ If you do get sick, stay home and rest! Wear a face mask if you must go out in public.

ENT infections can be painful and sometimes harmful. But thanks to your amazing immune system, science, and some healthy habits, your body is ready to face these germ **invaders**!

GLOSSARY

antibiotic—a substance used to kill germs that cause disease.

cavity—an unfilled or hollow space within a mass.

chronic—when something occurs frequently or for a very long time.

complication—a second condition that develops during the course of a primary disease or condition.

congestion—the state of having an excessive amount of mucus.

contagious—spread by direct or indirect contact with an infected person or animal.

genetic—of or relating to a branch of biology that deals with inherited features.

infect—to enter and cause disease in. This condition is called an infection.

invade—to enter and spread with the intent to take over. Something that does this is an invader.

organism—a living thing.

over-the-counter—available to purchase at stores without a doctor's prescription.

pus—a thick fluid that is usually yellowish-white and forms as part of an inflammatory response to an infection.

remedy—a food, medicine, or treatment that treats or relieves a disease or its symptoms.

sinus—a narrow, hollow tract in the skull that connects with the nostrils.

surgery (SUHRJ-ree)—the treating of sickness or injury by cutting into and repairing body parts.

symptom—a noticeable change in the normal working of the body. A symptom indicates or accompanies disease, sickness, or other malfunction.

tonsil—either of a pair of tissue masses on each side of the throat.

ONLINE RESOURCES

To learn more about ENT infections, please visit abdobooklinks.com or scan this QR code. These links are routinely monitored and updated to provide the most current information available.

INDEX

adenoids, 9, 20, 21
animals, 5
antibiotics, 12, 20, 24, 25

bacteria, 5, 6, 7, 12, 24, 25

cold, 6, 16, 18, 22
coughing, 6, 7, 16, 25, 28

doctors, 12, 13, 14, 18, 19, 20, 22, 24, 27

ears, 4, 6, 8, 9, 10, 11, 12, 14, 15, 26

face mask, 28
fever, 7, 10, 24, 25, 26
Fleming, Alexander, 12
flu, 16, 18, 22
fungi, 5

headache, 10, 25

immune system, 7, 22, 28

mold, 12

nose, 4, 6, 8, 9, 16, 19, 20, 25, 26, 28

over-the-counter medicines, 12, 18, 22, 25

penicillin, 12
plants, 5
protozoa, 5
pus, 14

remedies, 25
replication, 5, 7
rest, 12, 18, 28

sinuses, 6, 9, 16
sinusitis, 16, 17, 18
sneezing, 6, 7, 16, 25, 28
stomach, 8, 25
surgery, 14, 20, 21, 26
symptoms, 6, 7, 10, 12, 16, 18, 20, 24, 25, 26

throat, 4, 6, 8, 9, 22, 23, 24, 25, 26, 27
tonsillitis, 26, 27
tonsils, 9, 24, 25, 26
tubes, 11, 14, 15

viruses, 5, 6, 7, 12, 22, 24, 25

washing hands, 28
white blood cells, 7